Things I want to remember about this book!

_____

_____

_____

_____

_____

_____

_____

_____

_____

_____

_____

_____

_____

_____

(Quotes, Insights, Lessons, Ideas, Strategies, Inspiration,
Thoughts, Emotions)

UC
W BOOK BREAKDOWN

Book Title:

Book Author:

Purchase Date: **From:**

Finished Reading Date:

Book Type: ☐ Fiction   ☐ Non-Fiction   ☐ Other

Borrowed Book: ☐ **To:**

Book Rating: Bad! ☆☆☆☆☆ **Great!**

Describe this book in a few words:

Cost of Book:

"I think, Therefore I am"
- Rene Descartes

Things I want to remember about this book!

_____

_____

_____

_____

_____

_____

_____

_____

_____

_____

_____

_____

(Quotes, Insights, Lessons, Ideas, Strategies, Inspiration,
Thoughts, Emotions)

$^{UC}_{W}$ BOOK BREAKDOWN

Book Title:

Book Author:

Purchase Date: **From:**

Finished Reading Date:

Book Type: ☐ Fiction   ☐ Non-Fiction   ☐ Other

Borrowed Book: ☐ **To:**

Book Rating: Bad! ☆☆☆☆☆ **Great!**

Describe this book in a few words:

Cost of Book:

"I think, Therefore I am"
- Rene Descartes

Things I want to remember about this book!

_____

_____

_____

_____

_____

_____

_____

_____

_____

_____

_____

_____

_____

_____

(Quotes, Insights, Lessons, Ideas, Strategies, Inspiration,
Thoughts, Emotions)

UC
W BOOK BREAKDOWN

Book Title:

Book Author:

Purchase Date: **From:**

Finished Reading Date:

Book Type: ☐ Fiction   ☐ Non-Fiction   ☐ Other

Borrowed Book: ☐ **To:**

Book Rating: Bad! ☆☆☆☆☆ **Great!**

Describe this book in a few words:

Cost of Book:

"I think, Therefore I am"
- Rene Descartes

Things I want to remember about this book!

_____

_____

_____

_____

_____

_____

_____

_____

_____

_____

_____

_____

_____

_____

(Quotes, Insights, Lessons, Ideas, Strategies, Inspiration,
Thoughts, Emotions)

UC
W BOOK BREAKDOWN

Book Title:

Book Author:

Purchase Date: **From:**

Finished Reading Date:

Book Type: ☐ Fiction   ☐ Non-Fiction   ☐ Other

Borrowed Book: ☐ **To:**

Book Rating: Bad! ☆☆☆☆☆ Great!

Describe this book in a few words:

Cost of Book:

"I think, Therefore I am"
- Rene Descartes

Things I want to remember about this book!

_____

_____

_____

_____

_____

_____

_____

_____

_____

_____

_____

_____

_____

(Quotes, Insights, Lessons, Ideas, Strategies, Inspiration,
Thoughts, Emotions)

^{UC}_W BOOK BREAKDOWN

Book Title:

Book Author:

Purchase Date: **From:**

Finished Reading Date:

Book Type: ☐ Fiction   ☐ Non-Fiction   ☐ Other

Borrowed Book: ☐ To:

Book Rating: Bad! ☆☆☆☆☆ **Great!**

Describe this book in a few words:

Cost of Book:

"I think, Therefore I am"
- Rene Descartes

Things I want to remember about this book!

_____

_____

_____

_____

_____

_____

_____

_____

_____

_____

_____

_____

_____

(Quotes, Insights, Lessons, Ideas, Strategies, Inspiration,
Thoughts, Emotions)

UC
W BOOK BREAKDOWN

Book Title:

_____

Book Author:

_____

Purchase Date: **From:**

_____

Finished Reading Date:

_____

Book Type: ☐ Fiction   ☐ Non-Fiction   ☐ Other

_____

Borrowed Book: ☐ To:

_____

Book Rating: Bad! ☆☆☆☆☆ **Great!**

_____

Describe this book in a few words:

_____

_____

Cost of Book:

_____

"I think, Therefore I am"
- Rene Descartes

Things I want to remember about this book!

_____

_____

_____

_____

_____

_____

_____

_____

_____

_____

_____

_____

(Quotes, Insights, Lessons, Ideas, Strategies, Inspiration,
Thoughts, Emotions)

UC
W BOOK BREAKDOWN

Book Title:

Book Author:

Purchase Date: **From:**

Finished Reading Date:

Book Type: ☐ Fiction   ☐ Non-Fiction   ☐ Other

Borrowed Book: ☐ **To:**

Book Rating: Bad! ☆☆☆☆☆ Great!

Describe this book in a few words:

Cost of Book:

"I think, Therefore I am"
- Rene Descartes

Things I want to remember about this book!

(Quotes, Insights, Lessons, Ideas, Strategies, Inspiration,
Thoughts, Emotions)

UC
W BOOK BREAKDOWN

Book Title:

Book Author:

Purchase Date: **From:**

Finished Reading Date:

Book Type: ☐ Fiction   ☐ Non-Fiction   ☐ Other

Borrowed Book: ☐ **To:**

Book Rating: Bad! ☆☆☆☆☆ Great!

Describe this book in a few words:

Cost of Book:

"I think, Therefore I am"
- Rene Descartes

Things I want to remember about this book!

(Quotes, Insights, Lessons, Ideas, Strategies, Inspiration,
Thoughts, Emotions)

$^{UC}_{W}$ BOOK BREAKDOWN

Book Title:

Book Author:

Purchase Date: **From:**

Finished Reading Date:

Book Type: ☐ Fiction   ☐ Non-Fiction   ☐ Other

Borrowed Book: ☐ **To:**

Book Rating: Bad! ☆☆☆☆☆ **Great!**

Describe this book in a few words:

Cost of Book:

"I think, Therefore I am"
- **Rene Descartes**

Things I want to remember about this book!

_____

_____

_____

_____

_____

_____

_____

_____

_____

_____

_____

_____

_____

(Quotes, Insights, Lessons, Ideas, Strategies, Inspiration,
Thoughts, Emotions)

^{UC}_W BOOK BREAKDOWN

Book Title:

Book Author:

Purchase Date: **From:**

Finished Reading Date:

Book Type: ☐ Fiction   ☐ Non-Fiction   ☐ Other

Borrowed Book: ☐ **To:**

Book Rating: Bad! ☆☆☆☆☆ **Great!**

Describe this book in a few words:

Cost of Book:

"I think, Therefore I am"
- Rene Descartes

Things I want to remember about this book!

_____

_____

_____

_____

_____

_____

_____

_____

_____

_____

_____

_____

(Quotes, Insights, Lessons, Ideas, Strategies, Inspiration,
Thoughts, Emotions)

^{UC}_W BOOK BREAKDOWN

Book Title:

Book Author:

Purchase Date: **From:**

Finished Reading Date:

Book Type: ☐ Fiction   ☐ Non-Fiction   ☐ Other

Borrowed Book: ☐ **To:**

Book Rating: Bad! ☆☆☆☆☆ Great!

Describe this book in a few words:

Cost of Book:

"I think, Therefore I am"
- Rene Descartes

Things I want to remember about this book!

_____

_____

_____

_____

_____

_____

_____

_____

_____

_____

_____

_____

_____

_____

(Quotes, Insights, Lessons, Ideas, Strategies, Inspiration,
Thoughts, Emotions)

UC W BOOK BREAKDOWN

Book Title:

_____

Book Author:

_____

Purchase Date: **From:**

_____

Finished Reading Date:

_____

Book Type: ☐ Fiction   ☐ Non-Fiction   ☐ Other

_____

Borrowed Book: ☐ **To:**

_____

Book Rating: Bad! ☆☆☆☆☆ **Great!**

_____

Describe this book in a few words:

_____

_____

Cost of Book:

_____

"I think, Therefore I am"
- Rene Descartes

Things I want to remember about this book!

(Quotes, Insights, Lessons, Ideas, Strategies, Inspiration,
Thoughts, Emotions)

^{UC}_W BOOK BREAKDOWN

Book Title:

Book Author:

Purchase Date: **From:**

Finished Reading Date:

Book Type: ☐ Fiction   ☐ Non-Fiction   ☐ Other

Borrowed Book: ☐ To:

Book Rating: Bad! ☆☆☆☆☆ **Great!**

Describe this book in a few words:

Cost of Book:

"I think, Therefore I am"
- Rene Descartes

Things I want to remember about this book!

_____

_____

_____

_____

_____

_____

_____

_____

_____

_____

_____

_____

_____

_____

(Quotes, Insights, Lessons, Ideas, Strategies, Inspiration,
Thoughts, Emotions)

UC
W BOOK BREAKDOWN

Book Title:

Book Author:

Purchase Date: **From:**

Finished Reading Date:

Book Type: ☐ Fiction   ☐ Non-Fiction   ☐ Other

Borrowed Book: ☐ **To:**

Book Rating: Bad! ☆☆☆☆☆ **Great!**

Describe this book in a few words:

Cost of Book:

"I think, Therefore I am"
- Rene Descartes

Things I want to remember about this book!

_____

_____

_____

_____

_____

_____

_____

_____

_____

_____

_____

_____

_____

(Quotes, Insights, Lessons, Ideas, Strategies, Inspiration,
Thoughts, Emotions)

UC
W BOOK BREAKDOWN

Book Title:

Book Author:

Purchase Date: **From:**

Finished Reading Date:

Book Type: ☐ Fiction   ☐ Non-Fiction   ☐ Other

Borrowed Book: ☐ **To:**

Book Rating: Bad! ☆☆☆☆☆ Great!

Describe this book in a few words:

Cost of Book:

"I think, Therefore I am"
- Rene Descartes

Things I want to remember about this book!

_____

_____

_____

_____

_____

_____

_____

_____

_____

_____

_____

_____

_____

_____

(Quotes, Insights, Lessons, Ideas, Strategies, Inspiration, Thoughts, Emotions)

^{UC}_W BOOK BREAKDOWN

Book Title:

Book Author:

Purchase Date: **From:**

Finished Reading Date:

Book Type: ☐ Fiction   ☐ Non-Fiction   ☐ Other

Borrowed Book: ☐ **To:**

Book Rating: Bad! ☆☆☆☆☆ Great!

Describe this book in a few words:

Cost of Book:

"I think, Therefore I am"
- Rene Descartes

Things I want to remember about this book!

_____

_____

_____

_____

_____

_____

_____

_____

_____

_____

_____

_____

_____

(Quotes, Insights, Lessons, Ideas, Strategies, Inspiration, Thoughts, Emotions)

UC
W BOOK BREAKDOWN

Book Title:

Book Author:

Purchase Date: **From:**

Finished Reading Date:

Book Type: ☐ Fiction   ☐ Non-Fiction   ☐ Other

Borrowed Book: ☐ To:

Book Rating: Bad! ☆☆☆☆☆ **Great!**

Describe this book in a few words:

Cost of Book:

"I think, Therefore I am"
- Rene Descartes

Things I want to remember about this book!

_____

_____

_____

_____

_____

_____

_____

_____

_____

_____

_____

_____

(Quotes, Insights, Lessons, Ideas, Strategies, Inspiration,
Thoughts, Emotions)

UC
W BOOK BREAKDOWN

Book Title:

Book Author:

Purchase Date: **From:**

Finished Reading Date:

Book Type: ☐ Fiction   ☐ Non-Fiction   ☐ Other

Borrowed Book: ☐ **To:**

Book Rating: Bad! ☆☆☆☆☆ **Great!**

Describe this book in a few words:

Cost of Book:

"I think, Therefore I am"
- Rene Descartes

Things I want to remember about this book!

_____

_____

_____

_____

_____

_____

_____

_____

_____

_____

_____

_____

(Quotes, Insights, Lessons, Ideas, Strategies, Inspiration,
Thoughts, Emotions)

UC
W BOOK BREAKDOWN

Book Title:

Book Author:

Purchase Date: **From:**

Finished Reading Date:

Book Type: ☐ Fiction   ☐ Non-Fiction   ☐ Other

Borrowed Book: ☐ **To:**

Book Rating: Bad! ☆☆☆☆☆ Great!

Describe this book in a few words:

Cost of Book:

"I think, Therefore I am"
- **Rene Descartes**

Things I want to remember about this book!

_____

_____

_____

_____

_____

_____

_____

_____

_____

_____

_____

_____

_____

_____

_____

_____

(Quotes, Insights, Lessons, Ideas, Strategies, Inspiration,
Thoughts, Emotions)

UC
W BOOK BREAKDOWN

Book Title:

Book Author:

Purchase Date: **From:**

Finished Reading Date:

Book Type: ☐ Fiction   ☐ Non-Fiction   ☐ Other

Borrowed Book: ☐ To:

Book Rating: Bad! ☆☆☆☆☆ Great!

Describe this book in a few words:

Cost of Book:

"I think, Therefore I am"
- Rene Descartes

Things I want to remember about this book!

_____

_____

_____

_____

_____

_____

_____

_____

_____

_____

_____

_____

(Quotes, Insights, Lessons, Ideas, Strategies, Inspiration,
Thoughts, Emotions)

^{UC}_W BOOK BREAKDOWN

Book Title:

Book Author:

Purchase Date: **From:**

Finished Reading Date:

Book Type: ☐ Fiction ☐ Non-Fiction ☐ Other

Borrowed Book: ☐ To:

Book Rating: Bad! ☆☆☆☆☆ **Great!**

Describe this book in a few words:

Cost of Book:

"I think, Therefore I am"
- Rene Descartes

Things I want to remember about this book!

_____

_____

_____

_____

_____

_____

_____

_____

_____

_____

_____

_____

(Quotes, Insights, Lessons, Ideas, Strategies, Inspiration,
Thoughts, Emotions)

^{UC}
^W **BOOK BREAKDOWN**

Book Title:

_____

Book Author:

_____

Purchase Date: **From:**

_____

Finished Reading Date:

_____

Book Type: ☐ Fiction   ☐ Non-Fiction   ☐ Other

_____

Borrowed Book: ☐ **To:**

_____

Book Rating: Bad! ☆☆☆☆☆ **Great!**

_____

Describe this book in a few words:

_____

_____

Cost of Book:

_____

"I think, Therefore I am"
- Rene Descartes

Things I want to remember about this book!

(Quotes, Insights, Lessons, Ideas, Strategies, Inspiration, Thoughts, Emotions)

UC
W BOOK BREAKDOWN

Book Title:

Book Author:

Purchase Date: **From:**

Finished Reading Date:

Book Type: ☐ Fiction   ☐ Non-Fiction   ☐ Other

Borrowed Book: ☐ **To:**

Book Rating: Bad! ☆☆☆☆☆ **Great!**

Describe this book in a few words:

Cost of Book:

"I think, Therefore I am"
- Rene Descartes

Things I want to remember about this book!

_____

_____

_____

_____

_____

_____

_____

_____

_____

_____

_____

_____

(Quotes, Insights, Lessons, Ideas, Strategies, Inspiration,
Thoughts, Emotions)

UC
W **BOOK BREAKDOWN**

Book Title:

Book Author:

Purchase Date: **From:**

Finished Reading Date:

Book Type: ☐ Fiction   ☐ Non-Fiction   ☐ Other

Borrowed Book: ☐ **To:**

Book Rating: Bad! ☆☆☆☆☆ **Great!**

Describe this book in a few words:

Cost of Book:

"I think, Therefore I am"
- Rene Descartes

Things I want to remember about this book!

_____

_____

_____

_____

_____

_____

_____

_____

_____

_____

_____

_____

(Quotes, Insights, Lessons, Ideas, Strategies, Inspiration,
Thoughts, Emotions)

UC
W BOOK BREAKDOWN

Book Title:

Book Author:

Purchase Date: **From:**

Finished Reading Date:

Book Type: ☐ Fiction   ☐ Non-Fiction   ☐ Other

Borrowed Book: ☐ **To:**

Book Rating: Bad! ☆☆☆☆☆ **Great!**

Describe this book in a few words:

Cost of Book:

"I think, Therefore I am"
- Rene Descartes

Things I want to remember about this book!

_____

_____

_____

_____

_____

_____

_____

_____

_____

_____

_____

_____

_____

(Quotes, Insights, Lessons, Ideas, Strategies, Inspiration,
Thoughts, Emotions)

^{UC}_W BOOK BREAKDOWN

Book Title:

Book Author:

Purchase Date: **From:**

Finished Reading Date:

Book Type: ☐ Fiction   ☐ Non-Fiction   ☐ Other

Borrowed Book: ☐ **To:**

Book Rating: Bad! ☆☆☆☆☆ **Great!**

Describe this book in a few words:

Cost of Book:

"I think, Therefore I am"
- Rene Descartes

Things I want to remember about this book!

_____

_____

_____

_____

_____

_____

_____

_____

_____

_____

_____

_____

_____

_____

(Quotes, Insights, Lessons, Ideas, Strategies, Inspiration,
Thoughts, Emotions)

UC
W BOOK BREAKDOWN

Book Title:

Book Author:

Purchase Date: **From:**

Finished Reading Date:

Book Type: ☐ Fiction   ☐ Non-Fiction   ☐ Other

Borrowed Book: ☐ To:

Book Rating: Bad! ☆☆☆☆☆ **Great!**

Describe this book in a few words:

Cost of Book:

"I think, Therefore I am"
- Rene Descartes

Things I want to remember about this book!

_____

_____

_____

_____

_____

_____

_____

_____

_____

_____

_____

_____

(Quotes, Insights, Lessons, Ideas, Strategies, Inspiration,
Thoughts, Emotions)

UC
W BOOK BREAKDOWN

Book Title:

Book Author:

Purchase Date: **From:**

Finished Reading Date:

Book Type: ☐ Fiction   ☐ Non-Fiction   ☐ Other

Borrowed Book: ☐ To:

Book Rating: Bad! ☆☆☆☆☆ **Great!**

Describe this book in a few words:

Cost of Book:

"I think, Therefore I am"
- Rene Descartes

Things I want to remember about this book!

_____

_____

_____

_____

_____

_____

_____

_____

_____

_____

_____

_____

_____

_____

_____

(Quotes, Insights, Lessons, Ideas, Strategies, Inspiration,
Thoughts, Emotions)

UC
W BOOK BREAKDOWN

Book Title:

Book Author:

Purchase Date: **From:**

Finished Reading Date:

Book Type: ☐ Fiction   ☐ Non-Fiction   ☐ Other

Borrowed Book: ☐ **To:**

Book Rating: Bad! ☆☆☆☆☆ **Great!**

Describe this book in a few words:

Cost of Book:

"I think, Therefore I am"
- **Rene Descartes**

Things I want to remember about this book!

_____

_____

_____

_____

_____

_____

_____

_____

_____

_____

_____

_____

(Quotes, Insights, Lessons, Ideas, Strategies, Inspiration,
Thoughts, Emotions)

UC
W BOOK BREAKDOWN

Book Title:

Book Author:

Purchase Date: **From:**

Finished Reading Date:

Book Type: ☐ Fiction   ☐ Non-Fiction   ☐ Other

Borrowed Book: ☐ **To:**

Book Rating: Bad! ☆☆☆☆☆ **Great!**

Describe this book in a few words:

Cost of Book:

"I think, Therefore I am"
- Rene Descartes

Things I want to remember about this book!

_____

_____

_____

_____

_____

_____

_____

_____

_____

_____

_____

_____

_____

_____

(Quotes, Insights, Lessons, Ideas, Strategies, Inspiration,
Thoughts, Emotions)

UC
W BOOK BREAKDOWN

Book Title:

Book Author:

Purchase Date: **From:**

Finished Reading Date:

Book Type: ☐ Fiction   ☐ Non-Fiction   ☐ Other

Borrowed Book: ☐ To:

Book Rating: Bad! ☆☆☆☆☆ **Great!**

Describe this book in a few words:

Cost of Book:

"I think, Therefore I am"
- Rene Descartes

Things I want to remember about this book!

_____

_____

_____

_____

_____

_____

_____

_____

_____

_____

_____

_____

_____

(Quotes, Insights, Lessons, Ideas, Strategies, Inspiration,
Thoughts, Emotions)

UC
W BOOK BREAKDOWN

Book Title:

Book Author:

Purchase Date: **From:**

Finished Reading Date:

Book Type: ☐ Fiction   ☐ Non-Fiction   ☐ Other

Borrowed Book: ☐ **To:**

Book Rating: Bad! ☆☆☆☆☆ **Great!**

Describe this book in a few words:

Cost of Book:

"I think, Therefore I am"
- Rene Descartes

Things I want to remember about this book!

_____

_____

_____

_____

_____

_____

_____

_____

_____

_____

_____

_____

(Quotes, Insights, Lessons, Ideas, Strategies, Inspiration,
Thoughts, Emotions)

UC
W BOOK BREAKDOWN

Book Title:

_____

Book Author:

_____

Purchase Date: **From:**

_____

Finished Reading Date:

_____

Book Type: ☐ Fiction   ☐ Non-Fiction   ☐ Other

_____

Borrowed Book: ☐ **To:**

_____

Book Rating: Bad! ☆☆☆☆☆ **Great!**

_____

Describe this book in a few words:

_____

_____

Cost of Book:

_____

"I think, Therefore I am"
- **Rene Descartes**

Things I want to remember about this book!

_____

_____

_____

_____

_____

_____

_____

_____

_____

_____

_____

_____

(Quotes, Insights, Lessons, Ideas, Strategies, Inspiration,
Thoughts, Emotions)

UC
W BOOK BREAKDOWN

Book Title:

Book Author:

Purchase Date: **From:**

Finished Reading Date:

Book Type: ☐ Fiction   ☐ Non-Fiction   ☐ Other

Borrowed Book: ☐ To:

Book Rating: Bad! ☆☆☆☆☆ **Great!**

Describe this book in a few words:

Cost of Book:

"I think, Therefore I am"
- Rene Descartes

Things I want to remember about this book!

_____

_____

_____

_____

_____

_____

_____

_____

_____

_____

_____

_____

_____

(Quotes, Insights, Lessons, Ideas, Strategies, Inspiration,
Thoughts, Emotions)

UC
W BOOK BREAKDOWN

Book Title:

_____

Book Author:

_____

Purchase Date: **From:**

_____

Finished Reading Date:

_____

Book Type: ☐ Fiction   ☐ Non-Fiction   ☐ Other

_____

Borrowed Book: ☐ **To:**

_____

Book Rating: Bad! ☆☆☆☆☆ **Great!**

_____

Describe this book in a few words:

_____

_____

Cost of Book:

_____

"I think, Therefore I am"
- Rene Descartes

Things I want to remember about this book!

_____

_____

_____

_____

_____

_____

_____

_____

_____

_____

_____

_____

_____

_____

_____

(Quotes, Insights, Lessons, Ideas, Strategies, Inspiration,
Thoughts, Emotions)

UC
W BOOK BREAKDOWN

Book Title:

Book Author:

Purchase Date: **From:**

Finished Reading Date:

Book Type: ☐ Fiction   ☐ Non-Fiction   ☐ Other

Borrowed Book: ☐ **To:**

Book Rating: Bad! ☆☆☆☆☆ **Great!**

Describe this book in a few words:

Cost of Book:

"I think, Therefore I am"
- **Rene Descartes**

Things I want to remember about this book!

_____

_____

_____

_____

_____

_____

_____

_____

_____

_____

_____

_____

_____

_____

(Quotes, Insights, Lessons, Ideas, Strategies, Inspiration,
Thoughts, Emotions)

UC
W BOOK BREAKDOWN

Book Title:

Book Author:

Purchase Date: **From:**

Finished Reading Date:

Book Type: ☐ Fiction   ☐ Non-Fiction   ☐ Other

Borrowed Book: ☐ To:

Book Rating: Bad! ☆☆☆☆☆ **Great!**

Describe this book in a few words:

Cost of Book:

"I think, Therefore I am"
- Rene Descartes

Things I want to remember about this book!

_____

_____

_____

_____

_____

_____

_____

_____

_____

_____

_____

_____

_____

(Quotes, Insights, Lessons, Ideas, Strategies, Inspiration,
Thoughts, Emotions)

UC
W BOOK BREAKDOWN

Book Title:

Book Author:

Purchase Date: **From:**

Finished Reading Date:

Book Type: ☐ Fiction   ☐ Non-Fiction   ☐ Other

Borrowed Book: ☐ **To:**

Book Rating: Bad! ☆☆☆☆☆ **Great!**

Describe this book in a few words:

Cost of Book:

"I think, Therefore I am"
- **Rene Descartes**

Things I want to remember about this book!

_____

_____

_____

_____

_____

_____

_____

_____

_____

_____

_____

_____

(Quotes, Insights, Lessons, Ideas, Strategies, Inspiration,
Thoughts, Emotions)

^{UC}_W BOOK BREAKDOWN

Book Title:

_____

Book Author:

_____

Purchase Date: **From:**

_____

Finished Reading Date:

_____

Book Type: ☐ Fiction   ☐ Non-Fiction   ☐ Other

_____

Borrowed Book: ☐ **To:**

_____

Book Rating: Bad! ☆☆☆☆☆ **Great!**

_____

Describe this book in a few words:

_____

_____

Cost of Book:

_____

"I think, Therefore I am"
- Rene Descartes

Things I want to remember about this book!

_____

_____

_____

_____

_____

_____

_____

_____

_____

_____

_____

_____

_____

_____

_____

(Quotes, Insights, Lessons, Ideas, Strategies, Inspiration,
Thoughts, Emotions)

UC
W BOOK BREAKDOWN

Book Title:

_____

Book Author:

_____

Purchase Date: **From:**

_____

Finished Reading Date:

_____

Book Type: ☐ Fiction   ☐ Non-Fiction   ☐ Other

_____

Borrowed Book: ☐ **To:**

_____

Book Rating: Bad! ☆☆☆☆☆ **Great!**

_____

Describe this book in a few words:

_____

_____

Cost of Book:

_____

"I think, Therefore I am"
- Rene Descartes

Things I want to remember about this book!

_____

_____

_____

_____

_____

_____

_____

_____

_____

_____

_____

_____

_____

_____

_____

(Quotes, Insights, Lessons, Ideas, Strategies, Inspiration,
Thoughts, Emotions)

UC
W BOOK BREAKDOWN

Book Title:

Book Author:

Purchase Date: **From:**

Finished Reading Date:

Book Type: ☐ Fiction   ☐ Non-Fiction   ☐ Other

Borrowed Book: ☐ **To:**

Book Rating: Bad! ☆☆☆☆☆ **Great!**

Describe this book in a few words:

Cost of Book:

"I think, Therefore I am"
- Rene Descartes

Things I want to remember about this book!

_____

_____

_____

_____

_____

_____

_____

_____

_____

_____

_____

_____

_____

(Quotes, Insights, Lessons, Ideas, Strategies, Inspiration,
Thoughts, Emotions)

UC
W BOOK BREAKDOWN

Book Title:

_____

Book Author:

_____

Purchase Date: **From:**

_____

Finished Reading Date:

_____

Book Type: ☐ Fiction   ☐ Non-Fiction   ☐ Other

_____

Borrowed Book: ☐ To:

_____

Book Rating: Bad! ☆☆☆☆☆ **Great!**

_____

Describe this book in a few words:

_____

_____

Cost of Book:

_____

"I think, Therefore I am"
- Rene Descartes

Things I want to remember about this book!

_____

_____

_____

_____

_____

_____

_____

_____

_____

_____

_____

_____

(Quotes, Insights, Lessons, Ideas, Strategies, Inspiration,
Thoughts, Emotions)

UC
W BOOK BREAKDOWN

Book Title:

Book Author:

Purchase Date: From:

Finished Reading Date:

Book Type: ☐ Fiction ☐ Non-Fiction ☐ Other

Borrowed Book: ☐ To:

Book Rating: Bad! ☆☆☆☆☆ Great!

Describe this book in a few words:

Cost of Book:

"I think, Therefore I am"
- **Rene Descartes**

Things I want to remember about this book!

_____

_____

_____

_____

_____

_____

_____

_____

_____

_____

_____

_____

_____

_____

(Quotes, Insights, Lessons, Ideas, Strategies, Inspiration,
Thoughts, Emotions)

UC
W BOOK BREAKDOWN

Book Title:

Book Author:

Purchase Date: **From:**

Finished Reading Date:

Book Type: ☐ Fiction   ☐ Non-Fiction   ☐ Other

Borrowed Book: ☐ **To:**

Book Rating: Bad! ☆☆☆☆☆ **Great!**

Describe this book in a few words:

Cost of Book:

"I think, Therefore I am"
- **Rene Descartes**

Things I want to remember about this book!

_____

_____

_____

_____

_____

_____

_____

_____

_____

_____

_____

_____

(Quotes, Insights, Lessons, Ideas, Strategies, Inspiration,
Thoughts, Emotions)

UC
W BOOK BREAKDOWN

Book Title:

_____

Book Author:

_____

Purchase Date: **From:**

_____

Finished Reading Date:

_____

Book Type: ☐ Fiction   ☐ Non-Fiction   ☐ Other

_____

Borrowed Book: ☐ **To:**

_____

Book Rating: **Bad!** ☆☆☆☆☆ **Great!**

_____

Describe this book in a few words:

_____

_____

Cost of Book:

_____

"I think, Therefore I am"
- Rene Descartes

Things I want to remember about this book!

(Quotes, Insights, Lessons, Ideas, Strategies, Inspiration, Thoughts, Emotions)

UC
W BOOK BREAKDOWN

Book Title:

Book Author:

Purchase Date: **From:**

Finished Reading Date:

Book Type: ☐ Fiction   ☐ Non-Fiction   ☐ Other

Borrowed Book: ☐ **To:**

Book Rating: Bad! ☆☆☆☆☆ **Great!**

Describe this book in a few words:

Cost of Book:

"I think, Therefore I am"
- **Rene Descartes**

Things I want to remember about this book!

_____

_____

_____

_____

_____

_____

_____

_____

_____

_____

_____

_____

_____

(Quotes, Insights, Lessons, Ideas, Strategies, Inspiration,
Thoughts, Emotions)

UC
W BOOK BREAKDOWN

Book Title:

Book Author:

Purchase Date: **From:**

Finished Reading Date:

Book Type: ☐ Fiction ☐ Non-Fiction ☐ Other

Borrowed Book: ☐ **To:**

Book Rating: Bad! ☆☆☆☆☆ **Great!**

Describe this book in a few words:

Cost of Book:

"I think, Therefore I am"
- **Rene Descartes**

Things I want to remember about this book!

_____

_____

_____

_____

_____

_____

_____

_____

_____

_____

_____

_____

(Quotes, Insights, Lessons, Ideas, Strategies, Inspiration,
Thoughts, Emotions)

UC
W BOOK BREAKDOWN

Book Title:

Book Author:

Purchase Date: **From:**

Finished Reading Date:

Book Type: ☐ Fiction   ☐ Non-Fiction   ☐ Other

Borrowed Book: ☐ **To:**

Book Rating: Bad! ☆☆☆☆☆ **Great!**

Describe this book in a few words:

Cost of Book:

"I think, Therefore I am"
- **Rene Descartes**

Things I want to remember about this book!

_____

_____

_____

_____

_____

_____

_____

_____

_____

_____

_____

_____

_____

(Quotes, Insights, Lessons, Ideas, Strategies, Inspiration,
Thoughts, Emotions)

UC
W BOOK BREAKDOWN

Book Title:

Book Author:

Purchase Date: **From:**

Finished Reading Date:

Book Type: ☐ Fiction   ☐ Non-Fiction   ☐ Other

Borrowed Book: ☐ **To:**

Book Rating: Bad! ☆☆☆☆☆ **Great!**

Describe this book in a few words:

Cost of Book:

"I think, Therefore I am"
- Rene Descartes

Things I want to remember about this book!

_____

_____

_____

_____

_____

_____

_____

_____

_____

_____

_____

_____

_____

(Quotes, Insights, Lessons, Ideas, Strategies, Inspiration,
Thoughts, Emotions)

UC
W BOOK BREAKDOWN

Book Title:

Book Author:

Purchase Date: **From:**

Finished Reading Date:

Book Type: ☐ Fiction   ☐ Non-Fiction   ☐ Other

Borrowed Book: ☐ **To:**

Book Rating: Bad! ☆☆☆☆☆ **Great!**

Describe this book in a few words:

Cost of Book:

"I think, Therefore I am"
- **Rene Descartes**

Things I want to remember about this book!

_____

_____

_____

_____

_____

_____

_____

_____

_____

_____

_____

_____

_____

_____

(Quotes, Insights, Lessons, Ideas, Strategies, Inspiration,
Thoughts, Emotions)

UC W BOOK BREAKDOWN

Book Title:

_____

Book Author:

_____

Purchase Date: **From:**

_____

Finished Reading Date:

_____

Book Type: ☐ Fiction   ☐ Non-Fiction   ☐ Other

_____

Borrowed Book: ☐ **To:**

_____

Book Rating: Bad! ☆☆☆☆☆ **Great!**

_____

Describe this book in a few words:

_____

_____

Cost of Book:

_____

"I think, Therefore I am"
- Rene Descartes

Things I want to remember about this book!

_____

_____

_____

_____

_____

_____

_____

_____

_____

_____

_____

_____

_____

(Quotes, Insights, Lessons, Ideas, Strategies, Inspiration,
Thoughts, Emotions)

UC
W BOOK BREAKDOWN

Book Title:

Book Author:

Purchase Date: **From:**

Finished Reading Date:

Book Type: ☐ Fiction   ☐ Non-Fiction   ☐ Other

Borrowed Book: ☐ **To:**

Book Rating: Bad! ☆☆☆☆☆ **Great!**

Describe this book in a few words:

Cost of Book:

"I think, Therefore I am"
- Rene Descartes

Things I want to remember about this book!

_____

_____

_____

_____

_____

_____

_____

_____

_____

_____

_____

_____

(Quotes, Insights, Lessons, Ideas, Strategies, Inspiration,
Thoughts, Emotions)

^{UC}_W BOOK BREAKDOWN

Book Title:

Book Author:

Purchase Date: **From:**

Finished Reading Date:

Book Type: ☐ Fiction   ☐ Non-Fiction   ☐ Other

Borrowed Book: ☐ **To:**

Book Rating: Bad! ☆☆☆☆☆ **Great!**

Describe this book in a few words:

Cost of Book:

"I think, Therefore I am"
- Rene Descartes

Things I want to remember about this book!

_____

_____

_____

_____

_____

_____

_____

_____

_____

_____

_____

_____

(Quotes, Insights, Lessons, Ideas, Strategies, Inspiration,
Thoughts, Emotions)

UC
W BOOK BREAKDOWN

Book Title:

Book Author:

Purchase Date: **From:**

Finished Reading Date:

Book Type: ☐ Fiction   ☐ Non-Fiction   ☐ Other

Borrowed Book: ☐ To:

Book Rating: Bad! ☆☆☆☆☆ **Great!**

Describe this book in a few words:

Cost of Book:

"I think, Therefore I am"
- Rene Descartes

Things I want to remember about this book!

_____

_____

_____

_____

_____

_____

_____

_____

_____

_____

_____

_____

(Quotes, Insights, Lessons, Ideas, Strategies, Inspiration,
Thoughts, Emotions)

^{UC}_W BOOK BREAKDOWN

Book Title:

Book Author:

Purchase Date: **From:**

Finished Reading Date:

Book Type: ☐ Fiction   ☐ Non-Fiction   ☐ Other

Borrowed Book: ☐ **To:**

Book Rating: Bad! ☆☆☆☆☆ **Great!**

Describe this book in a few words:

Cost of Book:

"I think, Therefore I am"
- Rene Descartes

Things I want to remember about this book!

_____

_____

_____

_____

_____

_____

_____

_____

_____

_____

_____

_____

_____

_____

(Quotes, Insights, Lessons, Ideas, Strategies, Inspiration,
Thoughts, Emotions)

^{UC}_W BOOK BREAKDOWN

Book Title:

_____

Book Author:

_____

Purchase Date: **From:**

_____

Finished Reading Date:

_____

Book Type: ☐ Fiction   ☐ Non-Fiction   ☐ Other

_____

Borrowed Book: ☐ **To:**

_____

Book Rating: Bad! ☆☆☆☆☆ **Great!**

_____

Describe this book in a few words:

_____

_____

Cost of Book:

_____

"I think, Therefore I am"
- Rene Descartes

Things I want to remember about this book!

_____

_____

_____

_____

_____

_____

_____

_____

_____

_____

_____

_____

_____

_____

(Quotes, Insights, Lessons, Ideas, Strategies, Inspiration, Thoughts, Emotions)

UC
W BOOK BREAKDOWN

Book Title:

Book Author:

Purchase Date: **From:**

Finished Reading Date:

Book Type: ☐ Fiction   ☐ Non-Fiction   ☐ Other

Borrowed Book: ☐ To:

Book Rating: Bad! ☆☆☆☆☆ Great!

Describe this book in a few words:

Cost of Book:

"I think, Therefore I am"
- Rene Descartes

Things I want to remember about this book!

_____

_____

_____

_____

_____

_____

_____

_____

_____

_____

_____

_____

_____

_____

(Quotes, Insights, Lessons, Ideas, Strategies, Inspiration,
Thoughts, Emotions)

UC
W **BOOK BREAKDOWN**

Book Title:

Book Author:

Purchase Date: **From:**

Finished Reading Date:

Book Type: ☐ Fiction   ☐ Non-Fiction   ☐ Other

Borrowed Book: ☐ **To:**

Book Rating: Bad! ☆☆☆☆☆ **Great!**

Describe this book in a few words:

Cost of Book:

"I think, Therefore I am"
- Rene Descartes

Things I want to remember about this book!

_____

_____

_____

_____

_____

_____

_____

_____

_____

_____

_____

_____

_____

(Quotes, Insights, Lessons, Ideas, Strategies, Inspiration,
Thoughts, Emotions)

UC
W BOOK BREAKDOWN

Book Title:

Book Author:

Purchase Date: **From:**

Finished Reading Date:

Book Type: ☐ Fiction   ☐ Non-Fiction   ☐ Other

Borrowed Book: ☐ **To:**

Book Rating: Bad! ☆☆☆☆☆ **Great!**

Describe this book in a few words:

Cost of Book:

"I think, Therefore I am"
- Rene Descartes

Things I want to remember about this book!

_____

_____

_____

_____

_____

_____

_____

_____

_____

_____

_____

_____

(Quotes, Insights, Lessons, Ideas, Strategies, Inspiration,
Thoughts, Emotions)

UCW BOOK BREAKDOWN

Book Title:

Book Author:

Purchase Date: **From:**

Finished Reading Date:

Book Type: ☐ Fiction   ☐ Non-Fiction   ☐ Other

Borrowed Book: ☐ To:

Book Rating: Bad! ☆☆☆☆☆ **Great!**

Describe this book in a few words:

Cost of Book:

"I think, Therefore I am"
- Rene Descartes

Things I want to remember about this book!

_____

_____

_____

_____

_____

_____

_____

_____

_____

_____

_____

_____

_____

(Quotes, Insights, Lessons, Ideas, Strategies, Inspiration,
Thoughts, Emotions)

UC
W **BOOK BREAKDOWN**

Book Title:

Book Author:

Purchase Date: **From:**

Finished Reading Date:

Book Type: ☐ Fiction   ☐ Non-Fiction   ☐ Other

Borrowed Book: ☐ **To:**

Book Rating: Bad! ☆☆☆☆☆ **Great!**

Describe this book in a few words:

Cost of Book:

"I think, Therefore I am"
- Rene Descartes

Things I want to remember about this book!

_____

_____

_____

_____

_____

_____

_____

_____

_____

_____

_____

_____

_____

_____

(Quotes, Insights, Lessons, Ideas, Strategies, Inspiration,
Thoughts, Emotions)

UC
W BOOK BREAKDOWN

Book Title:

Book Author:

Purchase Date: **From:**

Finished Reading Date:

Book Type: ☐ Fiction   ☐ Non-Fiction   ☐ Other

Borrowed Book: ☐ To:

Book Rating: Bad! ☆☆☆☆☆ **Great!**

Describe this book in a few words:

Cost of Book:

"I think, Therefore I am"
- Rene Descartes

Things I want to remember about this book!

_____

_____

_____

_____

_____

_____

_____

_____

_____

_____

_____

_____

_____

_____

(Quotes, Insights, Lessons, Ideas, Strategies, Inspiration,
Thoughts, Emotions)

UC
W BOOK BREAKDOWN

Book Title:

_____

Book Author:

_____

Purchase Date: **From:**

_____

Finished Reading Date:

_____

Book Type: ☐ Fiction   ☐ Non-Fiction   ☐ Other

_____

Borrowed Book: ☐ To:

_____

Book Rating: Bad! ☆☆☆☆☆ **Great!**

_____

Describe this book in a few words:

_____

_____

Cost of Book:

_____

"I think, Therefore I am"
- Rene Descartes

Things I want to remember about this book!

_____

_____

_____

_____

_____

_____

_____

_____

_____

_____

_____

_____

_____

(Quotes, Insights, Lessons, Ideas, Strategies, Inspiration,
Thoughts, Emotions)

UC
W BOOK BREAKDOWN

Book Title:

Book Author:

Purchase Date: **From:**

Finished Reading Date:

Book Type: ☐ Fiction   ☐ Non-Fiction   ☐ Other

Borrowed Book: ☐ To:

Book Rating: Bad! ☆☆☆☆☆ **Great!**

Describe this book in a few words:

Cost of Book:

"I think, Therefore I am"
- Rene Descartes

Things I want to remember about this book!

_____

_____

_____

_____

_____

_____

_____

_____

_____

_____

_____

_____

_____

(Quotes, Insights, Lessons, Ideas, Strategies, Inspiration,
Thoughts, Emotions)

UC
W BOOK BREAKDOWN

Book Title:

_____

Book Author:

_____

Purchase Date: **From:**

_____

Finished Reading Date:

_____

Book Type: ☐ Fiction   ☐ Non-Fiction   ☐ Other

_____

Borrowed Book: ☐ **To:**

_____

Book Rating: Bad! ☆☆☆☆☆ **Great!**

_____

Describe this book in a few words:

_____

_____

Cost of Book:

_____

"I think, Therefore I am"
- Rene Descartes

Things I want to remember about this book!

_____

_____

_____

_____

_____

_____

_____

_____

_____

_____

_____

_____

_____

(Quotes, Insights, Lessons, Ideas, Strategies, Inspiration,
Thoughts, Emotions)

UC
W BOOK BREAKDOWN

Book Title:

Book Author:

Purchase Date: **From:**

Finished Reading Date:

Book Type: ☐ Fiction ☐ Non-Fiction ☐ Other

Borrowed Book: ☐ To:

Book Rating: Bad! ☆☆☆☆☆ Great!

Describe this book in a few words:

Cost of Book:

"I think, Therefore I am"
- Rene Descartes

Things I want to remember about this book!

_____

_____

_____

_____

_____

_____

_____

_____

_____

_____

_____

_____

_____

(Quotes, Insights, Lessons, Ideas, Strategies, Inspiration,
Thoughts, Emotions)

UC
W BOOK BREAKDOWN

Book Title:

Book Author:

Purchase Date: **From:**

Finished Reading Date:

Book Type: ☐ Fiction   ☐ Non-Fiction   ☐ Other

Borrowed Book: ☐ **To:**

Book Rating: Bad! ☆☆☆☆☆ Great!

Describe this book in a few words:

Cost of Book:

"I think, Therefore I am"
- Rene Descartes

Things I want to remember about this book!

_____

_____

_____

_____

_____

_____

_____

_____

_____

_____

_____

_____

_____

(Quotes, Insights, Lessons, Ideas, Strategies, Inspiration,
Thoughts, Emotions)

UC
W BOOK BREAKDOWN

Book Title:

Book Author:

Purchase Date: **From:**

Finished Reading Date:

Book Type: ☐ Fiction   ☐ Non-Fiction   ☐ Other

Borrowed Book: ☐ **To:**

Book Rating: Bad! ☆☆☆☆☆ **Great!**

Describe this book in a few words:

Cost of Book:

"I think, Therefore I am"
- **Rene Descartes**

Things I want to remember about this book!

_____

_____

_____

_____

_____

_____

_____

_____

_____

_____

_____

_____

_____

_____

(Quotes, Insights, Lessons, Ideas, Strategies, Inspiration,
Thoughts, Emotions)

UC
W BOOK BREAKDOWN

Book Title:

Book Author:

Purchase Date: **From:**

Finished Reading Date:

Book Type: ☐ Fiction   ☐ Non-Fiction   ☐ Other

Borrowed Book: ☐ To:

Book Rating: Bad! ☆☆☆☆☆ **Great!**

Describe this book in a few words:

Cost of Book:

"I think, Therefore I am"
- Rene Descartes

Things I want to remember about this book!

_____

_____

_____

_____

_____

_____

_____

_____

_____

_____

_____

_____

_____

(Quotes, Insights, Lessons, Ideas, Strategies, Inspiration,
Thoughts, Emotions)

UC W BOOK BREAKDOWN

Book Title:

Book Author:

Purchase Date: **From:**

Finished Reading Date:

Book Type: ☐ Fiction   ☐ Non-Fiction   ☐ Other

Borrowed Book: ☐ **To:**

Book Rating: Bad! ☆☆☆☆☆ Great!

Describe this book in a few words:

Cost of Book:

"I think, Therefore I am"
- Rene Descartes

Things I want to remember about this book!

_____

_____

_____

_____

_____

_____

_____

_____

_____

_____

_____

_____

(Quotes, Insights, Lessons, Ideas, Strategies, Inspiration,
Thoughts, Emotions)

UC
W BOOK BREAKDOWN

Book Title:

Book Author:

Purchase Date: **From:**

Finished Reading Date:

Book Type: ☐ Fiction   ☐ Non-Fiction   ☐ Other

Borrowed Book: ☐ **To:**

Book Rating: Bad! ☆☆☆☆☆ **Great!**

Describe this book in a few words:

Cost of Book:

"I think, Therefore I am"
- **Rene Descartes**

Things I want to remember about this book!

_____

_____

_____

_____

_____

_____

_____

_____

_____

_____

_____

_____

_____

(Quotes, Insights, Lessons, Ideas, Strategies, Inspiration,
Thoughts, Emotions)

UC W BOOK BREAKDOWN

Book Title:

Book Author:

Purchase Date: **From:**

Finished Reading Date:

Book Type: ☐ Fiction   ☐ Non-Fiction   ☐ Other

Borrowed Book: ☐ **To:**

Book Rating: Bad! ☆☆☆☆☆ Great!

Describe this book in a few words:

Cost of Book:

"I think, Therefore I am"
- **Rene Descartes**

Things I want to remember about this book!

_____

_____

_____

_____

_____

_____

_____

_____

_____

_____

_____

_____

_____

(Quotes, Insights, Lessons, Ideas, Strategies, Inspiration, Thoughts, Emotions)

UC
W BOOK BREAKDOWN

Book Title:

Book Author:

Purchase Date: **From:**

Finished Reading Date:

Book Type: ☐ Fiction   ☐ Non-Fiction   ☐ Other

Borrowed Book: ☐ **To:**

Book Rating: Bad! ☆☆☆☆☆ **Great!**

Describe this book in a few words:

Cost of Book:

"I think, Therefore I am"
- **Rene Descartes**

Things I want to remember about this book!

_____

_____

_____

_____

_____

_____

_____

_____

_____

_____

_____

_____

_____

_____

(Quotes, Insights, Lessons, Ideas, Strategies, Inspiration,
Thoughts, Emotions)

UC
W BOOK BREAKDOWN

Book Title:

Book Author:

Purchase Date: **From:**

Finished Reading Date:

Book Type: ☐ **Fiction** ☐ **Non-Fiction** ☐ **Other**

Borrowed Book: ☐ **To:**

Book Rating: Bad! ☆☆☆☆☆ **Great!**

Describe this book in a few words:

Cost of Book:

"I think, Therefore I am"
- **Rene Descartes**

Things I want to remember about this book!

_____

_____

_____

_____

_____

_____

_____

_____

_____

_____

_____

_____

_____

(Quotes, Insights, Lessons, Ideas, Strategies, Inspiration,
Thoughts, Emotions)

UC
W BOOK BREAKDOWN

Book Title:

Book Author:

Purchase Date: **From:**

Finished Reading Date:

Book Type: ☐ Fiction   ☐ Non-Fiction   ☐ Other

Borrowed Book: ☐ **To:**

Book Rating: Bad! ☆☆☆☆☆ **Great!**

Describe this book in a few words:

Cost of Book:

"I think, Therefore I am"
- **Rene Descartes**

Things I want to remember about this book!

_____

_____

_____

_____

_____

_____

_____

_____

_____

_____

_____

_____

(Quotes, Insights, Lessons, Ideas, Strategies, Inspiration,
Thoughts, Emotions)

UC
W BOOK BREAKDOWN

Book Title:

Book Author:

Purchase Date: **From:**

Finished Reading Date:

Book Type: ☐ Fiction   ☐ Non-Fiction   ☐ Other

Borrowed Book: ☐ **To:**

Book Rating: Bad! ☆☆☆☆☆ **Great!**

Describe this book in a few words:

Cost of Book:

"I think, Therefore I am"
- **Rene Descartes**

Things I want to remember about this book!

_____

_____

_____

_____

_____

_____

_____

_____

_____

_____

_____

_____

(Quotes, Insights, Lessons, Ideas, Strategies, Inspiration,
Thoughts, Emotions)

^{UC}_W BOOK BREAKDOWN

Book Title:

Book Author:

Purchase Date: **From:**

Finished Reading Date:

Book Type: ☐ Fiction   ☐ Non-Fiction   ☐ Other

Borrowed Book: ☐ **To:**

Book Rating: Bad! ☆☆☆☆☆ **Great!**

Describe this book in a few words:

Cost of Book:

"I think, Therefore I am"
- **Rene Descartes**

Things I want to remember about this book!

_____

_____

_____

_____

_____

_____

_____

_____

_____

_____

_____

_____

_____

(Quotes, Insights, Lessons, Ideas, Strategies, Inspiration,
Thoughts, Emotions)

UC
W BOOK BREAKDOWN

Book Title:

Book Author:

Purchase Date: **From:**

Finished Reading Date:

Book Type: ☐ Fiction   ☐ Non-Fiction   ☐ Other

Borrowed Book: ☐ **To:**

Book Rating: Bad! ☆☆☆☆☆ **Great!**

Describe this book in a few words:

Cost of Book:

"I think, Therefore I am"
- Rene Descartes

Things I want to remember about this book!

_____

_____

_____

_____

_____

_____

_____

_____

_____

_____

_____

_____

(Quotes, Insights, Lessons, Ideas, Strategies, Inspiration,
Thoughts, Emotions)

UC
W BOOK BREAKDOWN

Book Title:

Book Author:

Purchase Date: **From:**

Finished Reading Date:

Book Type: ☐ Fiction   ☐ Non-Fiction   ☐ Other

Borrowed Book: ☐ To:

Book Rating: Bad! ☆☆☆☆☆ **Great!**

Describe this book in a few words:

Cost of Book:

"I think, Therefore I am"
- Rene Descartes

Things I want to remember about this book!

_____

_____

_____

_____

_____

_____

_____

_____

_____

_____

_____

_____

_____

(Quotes, Insights, Lessons, Ideas, Strategies, Inspiration,
Thoughts, Emotions)

UC
W BOOK BREAKDOWN

Book Title:

Book Author:

Purchase Date: **From:**

Finished Reading Date:

Book Type: ☐ Fiction   ☐ Non-Fiction   ☐ Other

Borrowed Book: ☐ **To:**

Book Rating: Bad! ☆☆☆☆☆ **Great!**

Describe this book in a few words:

Cost of Book:

"I think, Therefore I am"
- **Rene Descartes**

Things I want to remember about this book!

_____

_____

_____

_____

_____

_____

_____

_____

_____

_____

_____

_____

_____

(Quotes, Insights, Lessons, Ideas, Strategies, Inspiration,
Thoughts, Emotions)

$\overset{\text{UC}}{\text{W}}$ BOOK BREAKDOWN

Book Title:

Book Author:

Purchase Date: **From:**

Finished Reading Date:

Book Type: ☐ Fiction   ☐ Non-Fiction   ☐ Other

Borrowed Book: ☐ To:

Book Rating: Bad! ☆☆☆☆☆ **Great!**

Describe this book in a few words:

Cost of Book:

"I think, Therefore I am"
- **Rene Descartes**

Things I want to remember about this book!

_____

_____

_____

_____

_____

_____

_____

_____

_____

_____

_____

_____

_____

_____

(Quotes, Insights, Lessons, Ideas, Strategies, Inspiration,
Thoughts, Emotions)

UC
W BOOK BREAKDOWN

Book Title:

Book Author:

Purchase Date: **From:**

Finished Reading Date:

Book Type: ☐ Fiction   ☐ Non-Fiction   ☐ Other

Borrowed Book: ☐ To:

Book Rating: Bad! ☆☆☆☆☆ **Great!**

Describe this book in a few words:

Cost of Book:

"I think, Therefore I am"
- Rene Descartes

Things I want to remember about this book!

_____

_____

_____

_____

_____

_____

_____

_____

_____

_____

_____

_____

_____

(Quotes, Insights, Lessons, Ideas, Strategies, Inspiration,
Thoughts, Emotions)

UC
W BOOK BREAKDOWN

Book Title:

Book Author:

Purchase Date: **From:**

Finished Reading Date:

Book Type: ☐ Fiction   ☐ Non-Fiction   ☐ Other

Borrowed Book: ☐ **To:**

Book Rating: Bad! ☆☆☆☆☆ **Great!**

Describe this book in a few words:

Cost of Book:

"I think, Therefore I am"
- **Rene Descartes**

Things I want to remember about this book!

_____

_____

_____

_____

_____

_____

_____

_____

_____

_____

_____

_____

_____

_____

(Quotes, Insights, Lessons, Ideas, Strategies, Inspiration,
Thoughts, Emotions)

^{UC}_W BOOK BREAKDOWN

Book Title:

Book Author:

Purchase Date: **From:**

Finished Reading Date:

Book Type: ☐ Fiction   ☐ Non-Fiction   ☐ Other

Borrowed Book: ☐ **To:**

Book Rating: Bad! ☆☆☆☆☆ **Great!**

Describe this book in a few words:

Cost of Book:

"I think, Therefore I am"
- Rene Descartes

Things I want to remember about this book!

_____

_____

_____

_____

_____

_____

_____

_____

_____

_____

_____

_____

_____

(Quotes, Insights, Lessons, Ideas, Strategies, Inspiration,
Thoughts, Emotions)

UC
W BOOK BREAKDOWN

Book Title:

Book Author:

Purchase Date: **From:**

Finished Reading Date:

Book Type: ☐ Fiction   ☐ Non-Fiction   ☐ Other

Borrowed Book: ☐ To:

Book Rating: Bad! ☆☆☆☆☆ **Great!**

Describe this book in a few words:

Cost of Book:

"I think, Therefore I am"
- **Rene Descartes**

Things I want to remember about this book!

_____

_____

_____

_____

_____

_____

_____

_____

_____

_____

_____

_____

_____

(Quotes, Insights, Lessons, Ideas, Strategies, Inspiration,
Thoughts, Emotions)

UC/W BOOK BREAKDOWN

Book Title:

Book Author:

Purchase Date: **From:**

Finished Reading Date:

Book Type: ☐ Fiction ☐ Non-Fiction ☐ Other

Borrowed Book: ☐ **To:**

Book Rating: Bad! ☆☆☆☆☆ Great!

Describe this book in a few words:

Cost of Book:

"I think, Therefore I am"
- **Rene Descartes**

Things I want to remember about this book!

_____

_____

_____

_____

_____

_____

_____

_____

_____

_____

_____

_____

_____

(Quotes, Insights, Lessons, Ideas, Strategies, Inspiration,
Thoughts, Emotions)

UC
W **BOOK BREAKDOWN**

Book Title:

_____

Book Author:

_____

Purchase Date: **From:**

_____

Finished Reading Date:

_____

Book Type: ☐ Fiction   ☐ Non-Fiction   ☐ Other

_____

Borrowed Book: ☐ **To:**

_____

Book Rating: Bad! ☆☆☆☆☆ **Great!**

_____

Describe this book in a few words:

_____

_____

Cost of Book:

_____

"I think, Therefore I am"
- **Rene Descartes**

Things I want to remember about this book!

_____

_____

_____

_____

_____

_____

_____

_____

_____

_____

_____

_____

(Quotes, Insights, Lessons, Ideas, Strategies, Inspiration,
Thoughts, Emotions)

UC
W BOOK BREAKDOWN

Book Title:

Book Author:

Purchase Date: **From:**

Finished Reading Date:

Book Type: ☐ Fiction   ☐ Non-Fiction   ☐ Other

Borrowed Book: ☐ To:

Book Rating: Bad! ☆☆☆☆☆ **Great!**

Describe this book in a few words:

Cost of Book:

"I think, Therefore I am"
- **Rene Descartes**

Things I want to remember about this book!

_____

_____

_____

_____

_____

_____

_____

_____

_____

_____

_____

_____

_____

(Quotes, Insights, Lessons, Ideas, Strategies, Inspiration,
Thoughts, Emotions)

UC
W BOOK BREAKDOWN

Book Title:

Book Author:

Purchase Date: **From:**

Finished Reading Date:

Book Type: ☐ Fiction   ☐ Non-Fiction   ☐ Other

Borrowed Book: ☐ **To:**

Book Rating: Bad! ☆☆☆☆☆ **Great!**

Describe this book in a few words:

Cost of Book:

"I think, Therefore I am"
- **Rene Descartes**

Things I want to remember about this book!

_____

_____

_____

_____

_____

_____

_____

_____

_____

_____

_____

_____

_____

(Quotes, Insights, Lessons, Ideas, Strategies, Inspiration,
Thoughts, Emotions)

UC
W BOOK BREAKDOWN

Book Title:

_____

Book Author:

_____

Purchase Date: **From:**

_____

Finished Reading Date:

_____

Book Type: ☐ Fiction   ☐ Non-Fiction   ☐ Other

_____

Borrowed Book: ☐ **To:**

_____

Book Rating: Bad! ☆☆☆☆☆ **Great!**

_____

Describe this book in a few words:

_____

_____

Cost of Book:

_____

"I think, Therefore I am"
- Rene Descartes

Things I want to remember about this book!

_____

_____

_____

_____

_____

_____

_____

_____

_____

_____

_____

_____

_____

_____

(Quotes, Insights, Lessons, Ideas, Strategies, Inspiration,
Thoughts, Emotions)

UC
W BOOK BREAKDOWN

Book Title:

Book Author:

Purchase Date: **From:**

Finished Reading Date:

Book Type: ☐ Fiction   ☐ Non-Fiction   ☐ Other

Borrowed Book: ☐ **To:**

Book Rating: Bad! ☆☆☆☆☆ **Great!**

Describe this book in a few words:

Cost of Book:

"I think, Therefore I am"
- **Rene Descartes**

Things I want to remember about this book!

_____

_____

_____

_____

_____

_____

_____

_____

_____

_____

_____

_____

(Quotes, Insights, Lessons, Ideas, Strategies, Inspiration,
Thoughts, Emotions)

UC W BOOK BREAKDOWN

Book Title:

Book Author:

Purchase Date: **From:**

Finished Reading Date:

Book Type: ☐ Fiction ☐ Non-Fiction ☐ Other

Borrowed Book: ☐ **To:**

Book Rating: Bad! ☆☆☆☆☆ **Great!**

Describe this book in a few words:

Cost of Book:

"I think, Therefore I am"
- **Rene Descartes**

Things I want to remember about this book!

_____

_____

_____

_____

_____

_____

_____

_____

_____

_____

_____

_____

_____

_____

_____

(Quotes, Insights, Lessons, Ideas, Strategies, Inspiration,
Thoughts, Emotions)

$\overset{\text{UC}}{\text{W}}$ BOOK BREAKDOWN

Book Title:

Book Author:

Purchase Date: **From:**

Finished Reading Date:

Book Type: ☐ Fiction   ☐ Non-Fiction   ☐ Other

Borrowed Book: ☐ To:

Book Rating: Bad! ☆☆☆☆☆ **Great!**

Describe this book in a few words:

Cost of Book:

"I think, Therefore I am"
- **Rene Descartes**

Things I want to remember about this book!

_____

_____

_____

_____

_____

_____

_____

_____

_____

_____

_____

_____

_____

_____

(Quotes, Insights, Lessons, Ideas, Strategies, Inspiration,
Thoughts, Emotions)

UC
W BOOK BREAKDOWN

Book Title:

Book Author:

Purchase Date: **From:**

Finished Reading Date:

Book Type: ☐ Fiction   ☐ Non-Fiction   ☐ Other

Borrowed Book: ☐ **To:**

Book Rating: Bad! ☆☆☆☆☆ **Great!**

Describe this book in a few words:

Cost of Book:

"I think, Therefore I am"
- **Rene Descartes**

Things I want to remember about this book!

(Quotes, Insights, Lessons, Ideas, Strategies, Inspiration,
Thoughts, Emotions)

UC
W BOOK BREAKDOWN

Book Title:

Book Author:

Purchase Date: **From:**

Finished Reading Date:

Book Type: ☐ Fiction   ☐ Non-Fiction   ☐ Other

Borrowed Book: ☐ **To:**

Book Rating: Bad! ☆☆☆☆☆ **Great!**

Describe this book in a few words:

Cost of Book:

"I think, Therefore I am"
- Rene Descartes

Things I want to remember about this book!

_____

_____

_____

_____

_____

_____

_____

_____

_____

_____

_____

_____

_____

(Quotes, Insights, Lessons, Ideas, Strategies, Inspiration, Thoughts, Emotions)

$^{UC}_W$ BOOK BREAKDOWN

Book Title:

_____

Book Author:

_____

Purchase Date: **From:**

_____

Finished Reading Date:

_____

Book Type: ☐ Fiction   ☐ Non-Fiction   ☐ Other

_____

Borrowed Book: ☐ **To:**

_____

Book Rating: Bad! ☆☆☆☆☆ **Great!**

_____

Describe this book in a few words:

_____

_____

Cost of Book:

_____

"I think, Therefore I am"
- **Rene Descartes**

Things I want to remember about this book!

_____

_____

_____

_____

_____

_____

_____

_____

_____

_____

_____

_____

_____

(Quotes, Insights, Lessons, Ideas, Strategies, Inspiration,
Thoughts, Emotions)

UC
W BOOK BREAKDOWN

Book Title:

Book Author:

Purchase Date: **From:**

Finished Reading Date:

Book Type: ☐ Fiction   ☐ Non-Fiction   ☐ Other

Borrowed Book: ☐ To:

Book Rating: Bad! ☆☆☆☆☆ **Great!**

Describe this book in a few words:

Cost of Book:

"I think, Therefore I am"
- Rene Descartes

Things I want to remember about this book!

_____

_____

_____

_____

_____

_____

_____

_____

_____

_____

_____

_____

_____

_____

_____

(Quotes, Insights, Lessons, Ideas, Strategies, Inspiration,
Thoughts, Emotions)

UC
W **BOOK BREAKDOWN**

Book Title:

Book Author:

Purchase Date: **From:**

Finished Reading Date:

Book Type: ☐ Fiction ☐ Non-Fiction ☐ Other

Borrowed Book: ☐ To:

Book Rating: Bad! ☆☆☆☆☆ **Great!**

Describe this book in a few words:

Cost of Book:

"I think, Therefore I am"
- **Rene Descartes**

Things I want to remember about this book!

_____

_____

_____

_____

_____

_____

_____

_____

_____

_____

_____

_____

_____

_____

(Quotes, Insights, Lessons, Ideas, Strategies, Inspiration,
Thoughts, Emotions)

UC
W **BOOK BREAKDOWN**

Book Title:

Book Author:

Purchase Date: **From:**

Finished Reading Date:

Book Type: ☐ Fiction ☐ Non-Fiction ☐ Other

Borrowed Book: ☐ **To:**

Book Rating: Bad! ☆☆☆☆☆ **Great!**

Describe this book in a few words:

Cost of Book:

"I think, Therefore I am"
- Rene Descartes

Things I want to remember about this book!

_____

_____

_____

_____

_____

_____

_____

_____

_____

_____

_____

_____

_____

_____

_____

(Quotes, Insights, Lessons, Ideas, Strategies, Inspiration,
Thoughts, Emotions)

UC
W **ADDITIONAL NOTES**

_____

_____

_____

_____

_____

_____

_____

_____

_____

_____

_____

_____

_____

UC
W **ADDITIONAL NOTES**

UC
W **ADDITIONAL NOTES**

_____

_____

_____

_____

_____

_____

_____

_____

_____

_____

_____

_____

_____

UC
W **ADDITIONAL NOTES**

_____

_____

_____

_____

_____

_____

_____

_____

_____

_____

_____

_____

_____

_____

_____

UC
W
ADDITIONAL NOTES

_____

_____

_____

_____

_____

_____

_____

_____

_____

_____

_____

_____

UC W "Bucket-List" Books

Here is a list of classic books you might want to add to your bucket list!

- ☐ **Don Quixote -** Miguel De Cervantes
- ☐ **Robinson Crusoe -** Daniel Defoe
- ☐ **Frankenstein -** Mary Shelley
- ☐ **The Count of Monte Cristo -** Alexandre Dumas
- ☐ **Jane Eyre -** Charlotte Brontë
- ☐ **Moby-Dick -** Herman Melville
- ☐ **The Portrait of a Lady -** Henry James
- ☐ **Huckleberry Finn -** Mark Twain
- ☐ **Ulysses -** James Joyce
- ☐ **The Great Gatsby -** F. Scott Fitzgerald
- ☐ **1984 -** George Orwell
- ☐ **Catcher in the Rye -** J.D. Salinger
- ☐ **Lord of the Flies -** William Golding
- ☐ **To Kill A Mockingbird -** Harper Lee
- ☐ **Catch-22 -** Joseph Heller
- ☐ **War and Peace -** Leo Tolstoy

UC
W "Bucket-List" Books
(Continued)

Here is a list of classic books you might want to add to your bucket list!

- ☐ **The Odyssey - ** Homer
- ☐ **Madame Bovary - ** Gustave Flaubert
- ☐ **Crime and Punishment - ** Fyodor Dostoyevsky
- ☐ **Pride and Prejudice - ** Jane Austen
- ☐ **The Sound and the Fury - ** William Faulkner
- ☐ **Great Expectations - ** Charles Dickens
- ☐ **The Grapes of Wrath - ** John Steinbeck
- ☐ **Invisible Man - ** Ralph Ellison
- ☐ **Les Misérables - ** Victor Hugo
- ☐ **Animal Farm - ** George Orwell
- ☐ **The Old Man and the Sea - ** Ernest Hemingway
- ☐ **Slaughterhouse-Five - ** Kurt Vonnegut
- ☐ **The Color Purple - ** Alice Walker
- ☐ **Howards End - ** E. M. Forster

Made in the USA
Las Vegas, NV
11 December 2021

37248938R00125